THE MODERN CHURCH
NEGRO

VAUGHN L. ADAMS JR.

©Copyright 2021 Vaughn L. Adams, Jr.

All rights reserved. This book is protected under the copyright laws of the United States of America.

ISBN-13: 978-1-954609-11-2

No portion of this book may be reproduced, distributed, or transmitted in any form, including photocopying, recording, or other electronic or mechanical methods, without the written permission of the publisher, except in the case of brief quotations embodied in reviews and certain other non-commercial uses permitted by copyright law. Permission granted on request.

For information regarding special discounts for bulk purchases, please contact LaBoo Publishing Enterprise at staff@laboopublishing.com.

Scripture quotations marked (NIV) are taken from the Holy Bible, New International Version®, NIV®. Copyright © 1973, 1978, 1984, 2011 by Biblica, Inc.™ Used by permission of Zondervan. All rights reserved worldwide. www.zondervan.com

Scripture taken from the New King James Version®. Copyright © 1982 by Thomas Nelson. Used by permission. All rights reserved.

The Holy Bible, King James Version. Cambridge Edition: 1769; King James Bible Online, 2019. www.kingjamesbibleonline.org.

Scripture quotations marked (NLT) are taken from the Holy Bible, New Living Translation, copyright ©1996, 2004, 2015 by Tyndale House Foundation. Used by permission of Tyndale House Publishers, Inc., Carol Stream, Illinois 60188. All rights reserved.

Scripture taken from The Voice™. Copyright © 2008 by Ecclesia Bible Society. Used by permission. All rights reserved.

Scripture quotations marked TPT are from The Passion Translation®. Copyright © 2017, 2018 by Passion & Fire Ministries, Inc. Used by permission. All rights reserved. ThePassionTranslation.com.

CONTENTS

Introduction 1

Chapter One: The Current Status
of the Black Church and what is to come 5

Chapter Two: The Pride and
Ignorance of the Church Negro. 11

Chapter Three: Envy/Selfish Ambition 19

Chapter Four: Love Loss for the People 29

Chapter Five: Identity Crisis:
"The Insecurity Within". 39

Chapter Six: The Cry of the People
"Looking for a Savior" 59

Chapter Seven: Savior, Precious Savior:
"The Solution" 79

About the Author 91

INTRODUCTION

The Black church in America has fallen away. Pursuing a true relationship with God now is pursuing the manipulation of the church's own people for selfish ambitions. Even in the Covid-19 pandemic, when most churches are physically closed or have been showcasing services virtually, the Black church and Black community still find a way to be at odds with one another. Selfish ambitions still linger on the horizon of our lives in the form of finance, relationships, power/status, and the sense of feeling important. Now I can't speak on the issues of churches from other cultures because I am not of those. I am a Black man in America who is writing to help liberate his people from the slavery in their minds, hearts and souls. Being set free starts with actually following God. We have gotten so wicked and filled with ignorance, thinking we are freeing people with emotional, rah-rah sermons and testimonies, but will turn right around and neglect that we have humanity we still deal with. We have Pastors, Bishops, Elders, and other clergy who will be holier than thou and be the nastiest individuals in life. The audacity these leaders have to prey on the minds of those seeking hope and manipulate them to believe Christ the way they believe, not letting them formulate a genuine relationship with Jesus! We have gotten so far from how God intends for the church to be in the world. God calls the church to be witnesses of Jesus around the world and show people a Godly way of living (Acts 1:8). We, in this generation, have gotten far from the heart of God. We as the Black church have turned the church into the den of thieves (Matthew 21:13). The house of God is supposed to be a place where prayer takes place, healing happens, restoration happens, and the transformation of people's lives takes place. Now in this generation we don't care about the things of God. It's funny, we say we want respect from white people and people around the world, but our actions say otherwise. We hate to be called niggers, but we constantly display nigger behavior. The idiotic negro behavior is an attitude that has to stop. Just think for one moment: We want Black people to be free from the slavery of their mind and soul, but you have a Bamma Negro Pastor leading a congregation of people to absolutely nowhere. Keep thinking about it for a moment: Some Pastors would rather have a wife, a side hoe, and money to fund the lifestyle he/she wants to

INTRODUCTION

live, instead of assisting the community that is crying out for help. This isn't an indictment on all Black churches. I have a great church family, but these are issues that plague the majority of Black Churches. Why listen to a man or woman who really doesn't care about your life? No wonder Black people are leaving the church or just not giving Jesus a chance. People in the church can be worse than people who are in the world. Believe it or not, the attitudes we exhibit are killing people and not saving people. As the church we may be the only representation of Jesus people may see, and we are out here acting like fools. I refuse to play the fool at any moment in life. We need to wake up and really live this life that God is calling us to live. That life is a life of holiness that shows who God is in our lives.

It doesn't matter the type of Black church; we all have the same issues that need to be addressed immediately. Whether African, Caribbean, or African-American, we all are facing the same issues in our churches. The Black church must to do better. Ask yourself these questions: Black people, do you even care? Do you care about your community? Do you even care about your family? You have an opportunity to destroy generational curses and gain generational blessings, but it starts with the way you live.

1 Peter 1:16 requires that we be holy. The reason we need to be holy is because we serve a Holy God. It is a mandate from God that we live for holiness. We are not living for perfection, but we live to pursue Holiness. When we are living for holiness, we are not consumed with mediocre living. We begin to live in a manner that God calls us to live. When we are distracted with status, appearance, and money, we neglect relationships we are supposed to have and we neglect the true work of ministry God calls us to.

CHAPTER 1
The Current Status of the Black Church and what is to come

> *And he taught, saying unto them, Is it not written, My house shall be called of all nations the house of prayer? but ye have made it a den of thieves.*
> St. Matthew 11: 17, KJV

For hundreds of years the Black church has been the voice and support for the Black community. Black folk for years would seek help from the Black church to evoke change to better the lives of African Americans. The Black community used to desire to help in various avenues such as education, social injustices and finances, just to name a few. For a long time now, it appears that there has been a disconnect between the Black church and the Black community. Somehow through the years there has been a shift in the atmosphere on what is important in life. That disconnect between the church and community is rooted in only gaining for oneself.

In Mark 11:17 (King James version), Jesus explains that the temple is a place for prayer, a place to reverence God, but the people were selling in the house of the Lord. Now I am always down for a great Christian book and other audio but when you start selling those things in the house of God that's a whole other issue. That was the very reason that Jesus flipped tables in the temple. People are coming to church for healing, for answers, for restoration—just overall for Jesus. People aren't coming to be sold to. We have Christian bookstores outside of church that can sell items.

People want and need love in this dying world.

The Black community is crying out that they need help and need it now. Due to the greed of officials in the church, it looks like they turned their backs on the community. The Black community needs help with things such as finances, strong advocates in the school system

CHAPTER ONE

(elementary, middle, high school and college), dealing with social injustice and much more.

People on the outside looking in feel like the church is asking for more and more offerings every Sunday but getting less and less involved in community service. Black people are fed up with churches saying, "Sow a $500.00 seed to the ministry and watch God bless you." How about this one: A guest pastor comes to preach at a church and says, "Form one line for those who can sow a $150.00 seed, form another line for those who only have $100.00 seed and the rest of y'all give what you can." How ungodly is that? How about when Pastors and Elders say, "God told me to tell y'all that if you sow a seed of $1000.00 you will reap a blessing like never before. God is trying to bless you in this season but you have to be willing to let God and let go." Now God wants to bless people in their appointed season of their life, but the elect of the church should not manipulate God and his word to get people to pay a certain amount of money to the church. This is a classic one to manipulate people to give all they have: "Some of you all have a stingy spirit in this church and that's why you're not blessed."

It is bad enough people are trying to get out of debt and break generational curses of financial despair. How wicked can you be to use clichés and try to make them sound Godly to draw money from a people who look to you to help them in their time of need? Then the elect of the church will bash people and say things like: "If they saved their money better, they wouldn't be in this mess." How can someone sit there and call people in the church stingy when the Black dollar goes to everything the church needs and wants? Even after all the bills are paid, they still hoard money that they can use to help people in their time of need. Don't get me wrong; there should be limits on how you help a person because some people are con artists, but the help you give a community isn't a one-time deal the majority of the time. The Black church, just like any other church, is in a great position to make a positive impact. It'd just rather be greedy for some wicked reason.

Due to increase of greed in the church, people take notice in the actions of church officials. People are not only just not coming to church; they are not submitting to Jesus Christ being Lord and Savior in their lives. People are now making up their own beliefs to fit what they want and need out of life. We the church are called to be witnesses (Acts 22:15) on having a genuine relationship with our Lord and Savior Jesus Christ.

CHAPTER ONE

When you are filled with selfish ambitions, greed, wanting to feel superior over your fellow man, that will lead to the stupidity of the decisions of the church elect. People now more than ever have lost hope and are now being led astray in other directions that don't point to God, and we as the church sit and look silly asking why? The answer is: It is us; we have to do better. We have to center our focus back on Christ and winning souls for him and not feeding the lust of the flesh.

Since we the church have operated in the flesh so much, we have completely neglected operating in the spirit. Being caught up in our fleshly desires we, for starters, miss out on the move that God is directing us toward. The majority of the time it's because we are neglecting the Holy Ghost. We get in a place where we make up things that sound good to tell people, instead of speaking to people at their needs and actually relaying what the Holy Spirit says to speak to the community. When we miss out on what the Holy Spirit is saying we can't get sound instruction on dealing with the needs of the people. Actually, neglecting the Holy Spirit is a sin. One of the functions of the Holy Spirit is to give us instruction for Godly living. Godly living requires us as believers in Jesus Christ to complete daily tasks in a Godly manner. When you are not listening to the Holy

Spirit, you're not even regarding what God is telling you to do. Not regarding God is like when your parent tells you to clean your room and you choose to do what you want, but get mad when your parent is upset over your disobedience. It is the same way when God is speaking to the church on the needs of the people but the church avoids the voice of God and then is dumbfounded when God is mad with the church and allows his wrath to take place and then wonders why the Black community is mad and not respecting the God we claim to have in us. Then they wonder why the Black community is straying away from the church. When people stray away from the church then they begin to stay away from Jesus altogether and look for things to believe in that fit their current situation instead of pursuing Jesus the Savior of our souls.

CHAPTER 2

The Pride and Ignorance of the Church Negro

> *Pride precedes destruction;*
> *an arrogant spirit gives way to a*
> *nasty fall.*
> Proverbs 16:18 (The Voice)

Ain't nothing like a prideful and ignorant nigga. Some people reading this will be caught up in their mind because I just said the word nigga, but in the Black church that's what a lot of us act like: just a bunch of niggas. The term nigger/nigga is an insult to Afro-American intelligence and character. Nigga/Nigger is just another way the rest of society classifies the Black community and the Black church. Black folk, just ask yourself this question: When are you going to stop participating in nigger behavior?

To the Black community, don't give up hope in God, don't let people's mental and emotional instability dictate who you are, and don't stop following after the Lord. I've been Black for a long time now and one thing I realized among Black culture is that Black people are very forgiving of other cultures but when it comes to forgiveness of our own, we tend to get irrational and unforgiving. Let another Black person offend another Black person, and it builds up animosity that carries for a lifetime. When there is so much animosity built up for one another it produces hatred, it produces resentment, and eventually it produces division among one another. When there is division then there is no true progression in life. Even in the Bible in the Gospel according to St. Matthew 12:25 it mentions that a house divided cannot stand. This is where we are in the Black community and as a Black church.

The Black community for years has looked up to the Black church for help, mainly financially, to help with social injustices—spiritual, emotional, and psychological help. Last, the Black community looked up to the Black church for positive role models. The Black church has failed in all these categories at least once, but it is ok; we are human and failure happens. You can't pay everyone's rent when facing eviction. You can't always

CHAPTER TWO

help every Black boy or girl who is wrongfully imprisoned or murdered by crooked police. It happens; you can't always help with those social issues because of the agreement you have with the church and law enforcement. It's understandable when you're too busy to just talk to people in your own community and help them deal with the stresses of life. All these things are understandable, right? Absolutely not. When you sign up to work for the Lord, Black church, you have a very heavy mandate over your life. You have the mandate to serve not just the church but those outside the church. Will you solve every issue of life? Certainly not, but while there is time you need to make an effort to serve those in your community and the world around you. When you're not serving what are you doing with your time? All you can do with your time is be useless. When you're being useless all you are caring about is self.

The Black church has gotten into a state where they are just caring about self. When you care about self you will find more useless things to indulge in. Think about it—what do people do when they have money left over after paying bills? They spend it on things they don't need instead of taking the amount left over to invest it in something productive. Not saying you can't treat yourself from time to time, but all the time is a tad bit too much. The Black church does exactly this same thing. It's nice to have guest pastors speak every once in a while, or have a special day to celebrate the church from time to time. The problem arises when you have to pay tons of money because you want to get a certain guest speaker for a particular day but neglect the needs of the community. Guest speakers are cool but you can't neglect the community. The community is in need, but people's pride and agendas are more important than the needs of others.

This is where people's pride comes into play and they miss out on God. The Black community gets prideful because they look to the church to help for a lot of things and get burned by the church. Eventually, if you keep getting burned it will lead to resentment, and then the resentment will lead to an eventual falling away from the church and its people. When people fall away from the church, they eventually denounce the faith. When people denounce the faith, they look for other modes of beliefs that fit their lifestyle, which ultimately enables people to live any kind of way.

Once the resentment of the church reaches its height the people denounce the faith and then speak false accusations against the church. A lot of Black people's hate/dislike for the Black church comes from a misrepresentation of Jesus Christ and what it means to be a follower of Jesus. What you see in a lot of Black churches is people who follow God for material things. Take, for example, when elders, pastors, and people in the congregation pray: They pray for God to bless them with things. Nothing is wrong with praying and thanking God for what he has blessed you with, but there should be more prayers thanking God for just being God. Just thanking God for giving his son Jesus so we can have a relationship with him and have eternal life is worth more than any material item you could ever possess. God isn't just a God who blesses us financially but he is God over every facet of our lives.

Now we have a people who were taught wrong about Jesus from the start. Due to false teaching of the reality of Jesus, the church capitalizes on that false teaching. Continued false teaching leads to abuse and after while a person will be tired of being abused. When you are tired of being abused you will attack the abuser to feel a sense of freedom. Once you feel free you will lack trust for people, places and things, mainly a lack of trust in people. When you feel like you can't trust anyone you will do everything in your power to achieve your own success and do it on your own terms. When you feel like nobody is helping you, now you feel like you don't need anyone, and you can make it by yourself. This is where the Black community is now; they have been so burned and abused by the Black church they can't trust them. When the Black community leaves the church, they feel they are more successful without the church, which then leads them to feel that they ultimately don't need God.

When you get to a place where you feel like you don't need God you are in a dangerous place. That dangerous place a person will experience is that they don't need God, and they will feel like their intelligence is superior to anything that pertains to God. Once you feel like your intellect is superior to the things of God then a person becomes wise in their own eyes (Proverbs 3:7). Then when you're wise in your own eyes a person turns to follow after wicked ways. At this point an individual becomes lawless, lacks decent moral composition, is overwhelmingly selfish, and can be cold and callus. This is the state a good portion of the Black community is in.

Due to more and more people in the Black community feeling betrayed and lied to by the church, and a sense of absolute displeasure for the church, Black people tend to find other ways to seek out spirituality. Once this happens people will often find the thing that suits the lust of the heart. Therefore, when you connect to things that just suit who you are it limits the growth of a person and can also lead to someone being stuck in their own ways of morality. When growth ceases it just leads to the demise of a person. That demise can be anything from self-hatred to hate for others to overall life of pain and hurt.

As the church we should never want to lead anyone to their own demise. You want to be an encouragement to people. Now don't get me wrong; at the end of the day, we are accountable for our own actions, but it's life's social interactions that impact the way we think and feel. There is no difference with the church. In the world we have heartache, pain, strife, suffering and much more life throws our way. When people come to church, they are looking for God, and to see the mannerisms of God operating through his people. The problem is people aren't really coming to Christ; they are coming to individuals who are trying to emulate Jesus Christ. Whenever you accept Jesus as Lord and Savior you should come to him and not to people. Jesus mentions in John 14: 16, "I am the way the truth and the life." Jesus is the way, not people. On the other hand, even though as the church we are not the way to salvation we are to walk according to the Holy Spirit and be a good example of how to follow Jesus Christ (Galatians 5:16, 1 Corinthians 11:1, Titus 2:7-8). We may be the only reflection that people may see and can be a factor in them accepting Jesus as Lord and Savior, but because of our pride and arrogance as the Black church we do the exact opposite.

In the Black church we get into places of prominence and power and begin to look down on those who are trying to get their lives in order. Those same people in our communities who are coming into church are challenging those people in power in the church because they know things should be better. Those so-called Bishops, Deacons, Elders, Trustees and all other respected positions in church can't handle their egos when they are challenged. We all should remain humble as we grow in life, no matter the position, but ultimately what happens is people are turned off by the church and will most likely not want anything to do with following the Lord.

CHAPTER 3
Envy/Selfish Ambition

> *For wherever there is jealousy and selfish ambition, there you will find disorder and evil of every kind.*
> **James 3:16, NLT**

One of the most critical personality traits that can destroy a church and also destroy the relationship between the church and the community is envy and selfish ideologies.

To the Black church, how do we get to envy each other instead of uplifting each other? We as the church know better and ought to do better. The world is watching our every move. We don't have the time to play these childish games. We are actually discouraging the community we are trying to uplift and bring into the body of Christ from partaking in a relationship with the Lord. In the Gospel according to St. Matthew 5: 14-16 we are called the light of the world and we are to let our light shine so the good deeds we do may give God glory. How is it we as the body of Christ would rather be wicked and let our evil deeds be shown? It's the wickedness of self that we display that hinders people from following the Lord. Instead of being a discouragement we have to be an encouragement, but it's our envy within that destroys a church, and then those on the outside looking in will not come.

The reason we fall into envy and discord in the church is because we want someone else's life and anointing versus working with those God has given us. A lot of times when you take your eyes off Jesus you end up focusing on the wrong thing. God has given us our own talents and uniqueness but because we wish we could be someone else we end up developing a jealousy toward that person.

Black people will literally think that the anointing someone has is so amazing they would do anything to have it. Having a gift like preaching, teaching, speaking in tongues, laying on of the hands and much more looks so glamorous in church. Before you desire to be like anyone ask yourself these questions.

CHAPTER THREE

First question: Where am I in the Lord? This question is very vital to our walk with Jesus. The most important thing we have in this life is Jesus. Without having a relationship with the son (Jesus Christ) we can't please the father (God). The only way to the father is Jesus (John 14:6). Therefore, ultimately, we need to repent of our sins and invite Jesus into our lives and our hearts (Romans 10:9-13). Once we are saved and establishing our relationship with Jesus, he will direct us to gifts and talents he has for us. Until then we shouldn't be worried about what we are going to do for the Lord. We also shouldn't want someone else's gift. That talent God has given is for an appointed time and all to glorify him. Each talent has its purpose in edifying the church (1 Corinthians 12). The gifts/ talents that God has given us are to be used to mature us as a church so we don't lack in serving God.

Once we have a better sense of where we are in Christ then we can see where we fit with roles. Then we can seek God for the role we have in the body of Christ. The next question we should ask God: "Lord, I humble myself to be used by you; what do you have me to do for you, oh God?" Not saying you have to say this verbatim but it's a start. It is extremely important we first humble ourselves before we do anything for the Lord. The step of humility is the one step that people miss and can lead to chaos such as envy, hate, and people stirring up strife within the church. When there is strife in the church especially the Black church, then you can't draw anyone to Christ. When people in the community sense strife from within the Black church then the Black community isn't going to listen to you. Remember, you're a representation of Christ. If someone sees you do bad, why would they want to listen to you? Black people are already hurt by Christianity since slavery, so therefore it's going to be extra hard to convince a community of people to believe in a Lord and Savior that allowed them to be enslaved by Europeans to build a society that will never care about them—a society that took verses from the Bible and manipulated them to keep slaves thinking slavery was normal. Those are the things the Black church has to keep in mind when we deal with our own. As Black people we are hurting mentally, emotionally, and spiritually. In order to do our part to heal the world, we have to take care of our own first, not neglecting everyone else, but we have to take care of our own people before we go out to do the business of the Lord elsewhere. Therefore, we cannot have strife between us in the church. We may be the only representation of Jesus people may see, so we have to represent Jesus well. We can no longer allow envy to consume us in the church.

CHAPTER THREE

The main issue we have when we envy one another is a twofold problem. The problems we have are the "I wish I had that anointing" and the "I can do better than them" attitudes. The "I wish I had that anointing" attitude usually leads many people into a world of trouble they are not meant to endure. We often fail to remember Jeremiah 29:11, NIV "For I know the plans I have for you, declares the Lord" God has a plan for each one of our lives. He has a plan of good and not evil, for a future and a hope, but what happens is when the desire to have someone else's anointing enters the heart, we often lose sight of God's promises to us. When we lose sight of God's promises to us, we slip into sin and forget the purpose God has for us. We have to stay focused on the plan God has for us because the plan leads us to the custom-made destiny for our lives. Therefore, the anointing(s) we are meant to have is because God created us specifically for this purpose. No matter how we view the gifts and talents bestowed upon us, God values it much more because he loves to see his creation thrive and glorify him.

The reasons people are led to wanting another person's anointing are, it looks cool, they want to be them, they want to make a profit from that particular anointing, and they desire the fame/attention of having that particular anointing. Be careful what you ask for. One of biggest lessons I learned in this life is to be who God called you to be. You never know the trials and tribulations that someone endured to be where they are in life. You may not be built to go through the things other people went through, because the mandate on their life had them go through certain things to get them to their destiny. When you try to go through the same thing someone else went through because you desire to be them, you will come to realize that because your anointing is for a different purpose, and not the journey you're forcing, you could end up crushed or even dead. The reason you survived the various things life threw your way is because God built you for that moment and had already written your story to win in that moment. Embrace the mission God has called you for and recognize that God values you and that is all that matters.

One of the other most dangerous mindsets to have is that you can perform someone else's calling better than them. The audacity of some negroes—they will see someone operate in their calling and will say within themselves, *I can do that, I would be better than them.* If you are the one who does this, please by all means repent and ask God for forgiveness. When you have this view of someone else's anointing, that you can do better, you're slapping God in the face. In other words, because of your envy, you feel like God made a mistake; God didn't know what he was doing. With this mindset a person feels like they know more than God.

When you have envy in your heart, that envy will produce conceit and a false sense of reality. A calling/anointing is not easy to obtain or to maintain. We don't serve a God who needs to repent of giving certain gifts/talents to certain people (Romans 11:29). Remember this: God has a plan. The plan that God has for you is for you and not for anyone else, and vice versa.

The ministry God has ordained for you is not about being better than someone else. It's about advancing the Kingdom of God throughout the earth and giving him the glory. It's the saddest thing in the world: People will see a pastor and say, "I can preach better than him," or see someone laying hands on someone and say, "I can do that plus more." Do you know how hard it is to pastor, to lay hands on people, to teach an array of other gifts? It is extremely hard to perform any gift God gives you. Whenever blessed with any type of talent you have to cater to that talent, and most importantly, check your spirit before you operate in the calling of God. With that being said, it is already a lot to deal with self, why worry about what another person is doing? God's got them under control; focus on the mandate God has on your life.

The other problem we have in the House of God is niggas being niggas in church. When typical negro activity occurs in the Black church, Black people don't want to come to church because of the ignorance of church folk. They see the circus that is operating in the church. The world is already filled with envy and hate, so why run to the church who is doing the same exact thing? It is absolutely too much to deal with the same behaviors in the church as you deal with in the world. Leave the world in the world and be the church that God calls you to be. When we keep the spirit of envy, especially the type of envy where you feel you can do stuff better than people God ordained to do it, you fall into having selfish ambitions that can lead to your demise and add to the chaos of the church. Once you start operating in your own agenda then you will ultimately miss the move of God for your life and you will reap the judgment that awaits you.

To my brothers and sisters in Jesus Christ, grow up and stop the nonsense. We are not in competition with each other; we are fighting against the powers and

CHAPTER THREE

principalities of wickedness in this world (Ephesians 6:12). The devil is out here trying to have his way with our community and we have to continue to fight the good fight of faith. Allow God's Holy Spirit to dwell in you richly so you can use the divine gift God has given you to advance his Kingdom. This life is bigger than you; it's about God.

CHAPTER 4
Love Loss for the People

> Numbers 20:4-10,
> 1 Peter 1:22, and 1 Timothy 6:10-12

When you are ministering in church you will come across a multitude of people with various issues. As a minister or any worker for the Lord, you take on a lot of issues, including your own. After a while you get frustrated, annoyed and may even experience anger. It happens to the best of us. Scripture says: "Be ye angry, and sin not" Ephesians 4:26, KJV. It is so frustrating—you can preach, teach, and guide people through the word of God and they still act ignorant. In the head of someone ministering unto someone, it is like you are giving the people the answers to an exam, and they still fail in life. It is baffling and frustrating to see the people you help overcome life's problems and they still fail. The question workers of the Lord ask when those around them are failing is: How? It is irritating to the soul. Witnessing this can be very discouraging and frustrating. As a minister for the Lord, you have a heart for the people and you want to see everyone win in life, but it just hurts so much to see people miss the mark. For some people it hurts so bad when they see people miss the mark, it causes some resentment toward the people. It may even cause the minister to have some love loss because of the anger and frustration of people not getting it, just not understanding God.

In the book of Numbers, we see that Moses journeyed with the people of Israel for a long time and because of their unbelief for many years, Moses was eventually fed up with the people. Pastors, Elders, Ministers, Deacons and anyone who works for the Lord deal with the unbelief of people. More times than often they deal with the unbelief of their own people, the disbelief of the saints. As a follower of Jesus Christ, you never want anyone to not believe in Jesus but it hurts when you have your own people who've been with you for a long time lose hope and forsake the faith. It is extremely frustrating seeing that because of all the words of encouragement, all the sermons preached, all the Bible study and Sunday school lessons taught and people still won't believe.

CHAPTER FOUR

Common questions a person may have when they feel like they've failed the people are: How did this come about for them not to believe anymore? And is it me, God? Where did I go wrong? Despite the questions we may have, God has an answer for all the questions we may have in our minds.

Let's start with the first question mentioned: How did this come about for them not to believe? In 1 John 2:19 it explains that if they had truly believed they would have continued in the faith, but this had to happen to manifest who is really of the faith. God is a God of revelation. He will never leave you in the unknown. God will reveal things in their appropriate time. God will reveal even those people who are not truly of this walk with the Lord unto us. The reason God let it be known who is not of this walk with the Lord is because God has places in this journey he is taking us and the places we are going aren't for just anybody.

Like the word mentions in Jeremiah 29:11, God has a plan for us that involves peace and not evil, a future and a hope. God reveals those who are not of the faith to us because God doesn't want his children to be subject to people who are dream killers and peace stealers. People who are peace stealers and dream killers are of the devil. The Gospel according to St. John 10:10 mentions that the devil comes to steal kill and destroy, but Jesus came that we may have life and have it more abundantly. Therefore, when someone or something is trying to subtract your peace and kill you, it is of the devil and not of God. One of God's desires is for you to live so he can bless you. In order for God to bless you he has to remove you away from the things that would kill you. To my ministers, elders, pastors, deacons and the whole body of Christ, stop blaming yourself for other people's shortcomings. You have your own walk with the Lord that you have to maintain. You can go to heaven or hell for yourself, not other people. Life is too precious to be worried with novice issues. Don't let the people dictate how you should love; have God be the dictator on loving people. A Pastor back home would say love God and love people. If we can focus more on loving God, we can be more efficient at loving people. God calls us to love our neighbor as we love ourselves (St. Matthew 22: 39). In order to achieve this love, we have to follow God's direction constantly and have the love of Jesus Christ living inside us—that love of Jesus mentioned in St. Matthew 22:39, "You shall love your neighbor as yourself." Overall, this love God is referring to is an enduring, everlasting love. With a godly everlasting love, you can have the ability to love those around you. Even on your worst day, when people frustrate your spirit, still love them anyway. As we labor in this journey you will come across all sorts of frauds and disingenuous people, and it's inevitable that we do so, but nonetheless, we still have to show a godly love toward them. We as the church can't waver in our love. If we waver in our love for people then we truly don't love. When we don't love the way God wants us to love then we are being disobedient. When our disobedience grows, it has us grow further away from the love of God and we end up putting a separation between us and God. When we separate ourselves, we end up growing coldhearted and that will affect how we treat those around us. To the body of Christ, I challenge you that you love people the same way you are expecting God to love you. The way we can actively love is through encouraging, gentle words, through sharing the Gospel, having empathy and sympathy, and overall showing Godly character at all times for the world to see. The journey is not easy. You will have constant backbiting all your life. Someone is always going to have something to say, but show them love regardless. Have compassion for those on the outside looking in because we were once hard to deal with; therefore, we the church should be compassionate to those on the outside because we needed the same compassion from God. Show love, no matter what.

Sometimes with the things we know about God we still may fall short in our thinking and have more concerns when people walk away from the Lord. The other question we experience is what did I do wrong? If you are still in disbelief as to where you went wrong, just pray. Actually, maybe you could've been more gentle with your words, or just maybe you could've been a better example of following Jesus. You will have a lot of maybes going through your mind. Of course, we wanted everyone to be saved, sanctified and set free, but in the wise words I heard in church, unfortunately, hell won't be empty. All you can do is make sure you do the right things so you don't end up there but, better yet, end up with the Lord for eternity. In making sure you're doing the appropriate things to please God, make it your duty to share Jesus with people and love on people. When in doubt, pray. Always pray in everything you do and everywhere you go. Pray in good faith, and just leave it in God's hands and he will do the rest.

It sounds so cliché — pray and leave it in God's hands — but it is true. I learned and continue to learn you can't change a soul. All you can do is either plant a seed, till the seed or water the seed. Whatever seed you are called to sow in someone's life, you sow it and leave the rest to God. Whenever we try to do more work than

CHAPTER FOUR

God, it leaves us feeling used up, fed up, dried up and more frustrated than when we started. If anything, we do more damage to ourselves and those around us when we put our extra touch on things.

Whenever we feel like we have to do more than what God has already ordained for us to do, it causes that individual to have unwarranted emotions that were never meant to be experienced or shared. We overall become emotionally driven and not God driven. We have to keep our emotions in check all the time. Keeping our emotions in check is a tough task. Some days are easier than others but it is essential to our wellbeing to check our emotions. It is very easy to cuss someone out. Deep down inside, it's actually refreshing. After giving someone a piece of your mind, you may feel like a weight has been lifted off your shoulders. Sometimes you'll feel bad, depending on your moral compass in life. Sometimes even as a follower of Jesus Christ there is always that one moment that can take you out of character and have you reverting to your old self. When you revert back to your old self, also known as your inner gangster, it will have you expressing yourself in an ungodly way. Now these moments will happen from time to time but we as Christians have to be wiser in identifying the situation and not falling into that temptation. Jude verse 24, KJV states that God is "[a]ble to keep you from falling and to present you faultless." God is so good he can keep you from falling. When God keeps you from falling that means any and everything. God can keep you from falling for the tricks of the devil and even pursuing any ungodly plan devised in the heart. It's up to the believer to just surrender to God. Take a look at Moses in the book of Numbers: a God-fearing man, a mighty man of God, and even he had his moments of frustration. Ministry is tough work but it's needed to advance the Kingdom of God all over the earth. You will experience many highs and lows but at the end of the day it is all to give God the glory. When we keep God, and not our emotions, at the center of our focus we have a better appreciation for God, for people, and for overall life. Don't let a moment cause you to delay your blessing or miss out on your blessing.

In Numbers chapter 20 you can see that Moses had a moment where he was fed up with the people once and for all. Later on in scripture you see that because of his frustration he missed going to the Promised Land. The reason for Moses missing the Promised Land was that he let his emotions rule over him versus leaving it in God's control. When you are someone who is very intelligent and just very understanding of a move of

God, it is hard to have compassion on those who don't understand like you. Moses had an excellent and accurate understanding of who God was, and where God was taking him and the people because of him having a relationship with God. As workers of the Gospel of Jesus Christ you want people to have the same understanding of God because you know how awesome God truly is. When people don't have the same understanding or lack thereof, it's frustrating and makes you not want to deal with people, and then leads you to lose love for people. We have to remember that we are to plant, till or water a seed, and God will do the rest. The key to appreciating growth is patience. We have to stay patient. Moses eventually lost patience, his emotions toward the people heightened and that led him to miss the Promised Land. How many times have we done endless work in a job, or marriage or even in the church but let one moment happen, and missed the promise? Some people were called to pastor but lacked patience and let emotions fuel them. They missed out on the promise. Some people would have had more success in everyday life but they let their emotions run their life and they missed out on the promise God had for them.

Don't be impatient but be patient in everything. Don't let your emotions fuel your passion for the Lord but let

God through the power of the Holy Spirit reign within you. When you do so, you can reap the promise of God to its fullest.

CHAPTER 5
Identity Crisis: "The Insecurity Within"

> Ephesians 6:11-12, and
> Jeremiah 29:11

When ministering unto the people in or out of church we have to remember that the people are not our enemy; it is the spirits of darkness of this present age that cause the anxieties of life which will lead to a crisis of our identity. An identity crisis will lead individuals to having insecurity within. When someone deals with insecurity, that can eventually lead to various anxieties in one's life. We all have insecurity that plagues the mind and soul, such as physical (the way you look), emotional (the feelings you dwell within), psychological (the thoughts of the mind), relational (how we perceive the way others feel about us, and the feelings we exchange in return), and financial anxieties.

The greatest battles we all exhibit in our everyday lives are those of psychological anxieties. When we let our thoughts overtake us, that will ultimately control how we feel about everything that embodies our very existence. To overcome insecurity, we need to know ourselves; we have to know the creator, and what I mean by knowing the creator is to know God. To know God, you have to have a relationship with him. The way to get that relationship is to accept his son Jesus Christ as Lord and Savior. This is the only way to know oneself. When you are not in Christ you are living for the world and society molds you into who the world wants you to be. The way the world molds you is not your true identity. When you put your identity in Christ, the Lord will show you who you are and where you are going. God will show you where you're going in life and will mold your character for his glory.

There are quite a number of problems we have with identity in the Black church. Of course, the problems we acquired didn't begin in church; they began when Blacks were slaves being stripped of their heritage, being brainwashed of a true relationship of Jesus

Christ by removing scripture to convince African slaves that this was God's will. Those experiences from slavery alone were the root cause why for generations we haven't known ourselves. We keep passing on the generational curse of the lack of identity. The time is now where we don't just know ourselves, but we know who God calls us to be.

Here are some steps in knowing your worth in who God called you to be.

Step 1: 1 Peter 2: 9 - You are chosen, you are special to God.

People who deal with insecurities want to feel special. They desire to feel needed and God wants us to know that we are special; we are his prized possession. 1 Peter 2:9 teaches us that we are chosen, royalty and his special people. Often we will feel insecure about ourselves because in our day-to-day living, we as individuals will feel inadequate because of how we perceive we are being treated in the world. Our outlook on life shapes our reality. Sometimes we look so much on the abuse verbally, mentally, emotionally, financially, physically and spiritually it drains us and we feel unappreciated. No matter if you are a man or a woman, we desire to be appreciated and loved. When there is a lack of appreciation and love we go elsewhere to find it.

In our humanity we will seek different avenues to feel appreciated. Where we are in life it will dictate the avenue in which we seek love. Some of us will try to find it in our careers, some in relationships, whether dating or in friends, or sometimes we seek to find value in ourselves, in physical activities. By participating in humanity, we want to know that our existence is warranted. To show appreciation we want some sort of recognition such as rewards or words of praise. Once the praise for who we are stops we begin trying to explore options of other places to be praised. Eventually the recognition stops; now we observe things differently, which will lead to us being in a depressed state of mind and that will lead to insecurities we carry in our everyday interactions. When we carry depression with us it clouds the judgments we make; therefore, we end up in bad relationships, make terrible financial decisions and bad career moves, and then feel stuck, with no way out.

In the Black community when we feel like there is no love within, no love/appreciation from those around us, we decide to come to church to prove our self- worth. The problem arises when we are coming to church to heal us instead of coming to Jesus. Individuals will come to be healed from the abuse of life. There is a lot of abuse people take living in this world: financial, physical, and emotional abuse to name a few. Once the person feels rejuvenated, they begin the process of growth. As they are growing in the church, they gain different positions of authority. Now when given power in church that role will become that person's identity. There is more to a person than the role they play in church. One problem we have to first identify is that you don't just come to church to get your identity. You come to encounter Jesus. A lot of times we want people to validate our very existence. Mind you, Proverbs 27:2, NIV says, "Let another praise you, and not your own mouth". That verse in context means not to boast on things you do, but let the words of others give you the recognition. That verse doesn't mean the words of people will be the end-all and be-all. If anything, the Gospel according to St. Matthew 5:11, NIV says, "Blessed are you when people insult you, persecute you and falsely say all kinds of evil against you because of me." Therefore, for this reason alone we can't let people dictate our true identity. People's emotions can be unstable. One minute people praise you and the next minute the people hate you and will defame your name. As a people we need to realize the church is within us.

It is not the walls of the church that make us followers of Jesus Christ, but it is the spirit of the Lord that makes us who we are truly are. Now I'm not saying don't go to church, because church fellowship is essential to the soul. We are human; we need to fellowship with each other. That's how we grow emotionally, psychologically, and spiritually. Proverbs 18:1, NKJV says, "A man who isolates himself seeks his own desires; rages against all wise judgment." Without having social interaction, we will hinder who God intended us to be and are led away to indulge in wicked desires. Therefore, church is good but church is not the essence of who we are. Our relationship with Jesus is who we are.

We become so consumed with how the church labels us as a people we forget who God says we are in his word. To the Black church around the world, stop belittling your own people. A person's word is not the end-all and be-all on your life. Due to the effects of slavery, we've been indoctrinated to treat each other as inferior, because of socio-economic status. We are operating from a past mindset instead of moving forward to be liberated and free.

In slavery the house negro was the negro that made it to a better status. He still had no identity but he felt better

CHAPTER FIVE

because he was not in the fields doing hard labor. The house negro then felt a sense of superiority because his master allowed him to feel this way because he was not where he used to be, therefore he looked down on those who were still slaving in the field, even though he himself was still a slave, just in a better place. This is where we are as the church and the Black community. The elect of the church have risen above their life circumstances just to play the house nigger and to feel good about themselves because someone makes them feel good by hearing a person's eisegesis of God's word instead of the exegesis. Now hearing a false interpretation of God's word, church folk will cling to what sounds good instead of what's good and true. When we do that, we are allowing people to dictate how we should feel and act versus what God says we should do and how we should act. When we continue to live in this manner, we eventually will end up back at the point where we first were when we came to church, not knowing who we are.

It is imperative to keep in mind that despite what people in church feel or people in the world may tell us, God views us as special. We as believers in Christ have to look within ourselves and keep that at the forefront of our minds. Philippians 4:8, NKJV explains we should think on the true things, the noble, the just, the pure, lovely and things of good report. When you think on those things you will stay in consistent remembrance of who God says you are. You will then know the affection that God has for you. Knowing God's affection toward you will let you know that you are special, you are worthy, you are set apart, and you are his chosen royalty.

Step 2: 1 Corinthians 15:33 and Matthew 5:30 - Cut off the wicked

Once you know who God calls you to be and the affection God has for you, then the next step is knowing your identity in Christ. When in Christ we are called to be set apart, not to conform to the worldly views, but to be transformed in our mind (Romans 12:2). When we as a people achieve transformation in Christ, we need to cut off toxic people, places and things from our life. If we don't permanently separate ourselves from toxicity in our lives, it will hinder us from growing in Christ. When our growth is hindered, it hinders us as a people from experiencing a true and genuine relationship with Jesus. Picture being in a relationship with someone you love and trying to grow with them, yet you have toxic people in your corner advising your relationship. What will eventually happen is it will add confusion to a person's life. Over time it can cause tension in the relationship because of the advice of the wicked. That advice will lead to insecurities which will block growth and will lead to the eventual demise of the relationship. The same way we can't dwell in toxic environments to grow our beloved human relationships is the same way we can't remain in toxic situations to grow our relationship with Jesus Christ. Therefore, we ought to separate ourselves from toxic people, places and things so we can consistently grow in Christ.

As a people the reason we don't thrive in our relationship with Jesus Christ is because we focus too much on the hindrances rather than fixing our eyes on Jesus. When our eyes are not on Jesus we can't connect with the Father because we are blinded with the corruption of character that has befallen us. 1 Corinthians 15:33, TPT says, "Stop fooling ourselves! Evil companions will corrupt good morals and character." Just because we are in the spirit doesn't mean we can't fall victim to our character reaping corruption if we are not careful. The beauty is, we serve a God that can keep us from falling (Jude 1:24), but we have to make a concerted effort to seek after Jesus. When we seek him, then he keeps us from slipping. When we have toxic relationships around us it clouds our judgment and leads us to destruction. According to a post from Keck Medicine from the University of Southern California, researchers say, "Toxic relationships are tied to psychological condition idealization." Idealization is when an individual presents something or searches for something perfect. As a society we tend to search for the ideal relationship. It is natural to desire some form of relationship. Relationships give us a sense of knowing we are valued and wanted. All of our human existence we seek to be appreciated and loved. Therefore, as we seek approval from others we set some realistic parameters on the relationships, and some unrealistic expectations for relationships. In the Black community we tend to set expectations based on past hurts or on what some religious person has spoken. One of the problems with that is when we live off of past hurt it clouds our judgment regarding who God really is. When we carry pain from the past, we subconsciously have a negative view of how we ought to live for Jesus. That negative view leads us to gravitate toward an eisegesis of the word of God instead of an exegesis of God's word. An exegesis is an accurate, Holy Spirit revealed explanation of God's word. With a clouded mind it's hard to truly receive what God is conveying to us on a personal level. When we can't receive God personally, we will engage in creating idealized situations personally and theologically. The way we view God is how we will view ourselves and others around us. Therefore, it is critical we have a true relationship with God. If not, we create thought patterns of what a perfect church dynamic should resemble. We will create unrealistic expectations of the children of God and we create unrealistic expectations of how God should operate in our lives. The majority of the time, if not all the time, these ideal situations will fail us at one point or another.

Once we separate ourselves from the idea of relationships being ideal, we as individuals can make better decisions in choosing the right relationships and can value those relationship for their purposes in our lives. When we can truly value the relationship instead of making it the perfection situation, we can grow in wisdom and understanding of life. I find this true even in the church. Growing up as the child of a pastor I witnessed a multitude of behaviors that didn't make sense as a child. I would see people profess their love for the Lord in church but then would see the same deacons, lay leaders, ushers, ministers and other clergy outside of church act as if they had no regard to live a life pleasing to God. Therefore, I was conflicted in the dynamic of church behavior and being a Christian. Once I became an adult and received Jesus as Lord and

Savior, I realized that the relationships I experienced in life wouldn't be perfect. We all have our flaws but we are here to help each other. We can't make it in this world on our own; we need each other. Relationships such as friendships, co-workers, romantic relationships, and even family will bring out the best of the best in us by pruning out the worst part of us. God uses the people in our lives so we will grow.

As we engage in various relationships, we still have to be aware of the people we deal with on a daily basis. Just because we have the Holy Spirit living inside us doesn't mean we are meant to cater to just any- and everyone. God has divine connections for our lives but we need to get out of our own way in seeking the ideal situation. When we seek ideal/perfect encounters we will be more likely to end up with people who are toxic for us. This is especially true for attending a particular church. Not all churches are good churches. Not all churches are seeking Jesus. Seeking the ideal situation will have you in the wrong surroundings. Those wrong surroundings will lead to experiencing hurt that you were never meant to experience and to a negative outlook on life. That negative outlook can eventually lead a person astray from Christ. The goal is not to be led astray but to be led closer to Christ. To those who are

CHAPTER FIVE

seeking a savior, Jesus Christ is the way. Don't seek an ideal Christian and make them the ultimate standard of Christianity. It is impossible to be perfect in our lives, therefore no one person can be a perfect Christian. When we put someone on a pedestal, we make them our idol. When you are making someone your idol you are making them your God. Exodus 20: 3 (NKJV) says when you make someone your God, you're putting them in front of the one True God. God's desire is to have your full attention and to have your full love. God gave us Jesus Christ so we can experience real love. To experience God, we have to embrace his love and his love alone; everything else will follow. God has given us examples of Godly living in scripture (Hebrews 12:1). The examples given to us show how we live a life pleasing to God no matter the situation, but they are not to be made to be God for us. Therefore, we must not follow men because we are flawed and constantly evolving, yet follow the one who is complete in every way—our Lord and Savior Jesus Christ. Jesus is the way and we must follow him even in our relationships so we can be victorious in our daily lives.

To the body of Christ, I urge and encourage you to stop creating false representations of Christ through inaccurate hermeneutics of scripture and living a contradictory

Christian life. The people are crying out for help. They need a savior in Jesus but get frustrated because of the life we are living. Like I mentioned before, we are not to be idolized because that makes us God when there is only one true God. The mission is to win souls to Christ; that way people may be liberated and free, not chained and bound to the slavery of their sins. The way we represent Christ is the way the people on the outside looking in will view Christ and base their identity in Jesus. The way people base their identity in Christ is how they cater to their relationship with God and how they will cater to their relationship with those around them. Therefore, saints, remember we are ambassadors for Jesus. The world is watching so let's live for God with honesty and integrity.

Step 3: Learn about God and love on God.

The key to this journey in knowing self and your identity in Christ is to get to know and to love God. The way you view God is how you view yourself, how you treat yourself, how you view others and how you are going to treat others. You can't know yourself and treat others with love until you know God. The way you know the essence of God is to build a relationship with God. To build that relationship with God is to first accept

CHAPTER FIVE

his son Jesus Christ as your Lord and Savior, through repentance and inviting him into your heart. Then you grow in your relationship through reading the Bible, prayer and worship. To know in depth who God is, it is essential to read God's word. It is God's word that allows us to know the essence of him and our identity in Christ. 2 Timothy 2:15-16 explains that we should study and constantly seek God. It is the word of God that brings clarity to our lives and gives us the direction on how we should live to please God. In this world we will encounter various trials and temptations and we need the word of God to press our way through.

The problem arises when we learn about God but we don't accurately learn who God is. It is not enough just to learn about God; it is essential that we accurately understand who God is. In the Black community we have a tendency to self-teach ourselves the word of God, which can cause us to have biased feelings regarding Christianity. When a person has biases on what is being taught about God it can cloud that person's judgment on how to live for Jesus, and that clouded judgment can lead to a hindrance in growth, which will lead to hindrance in knowing your identity in Christ. If you don't know who you are in Christ you won't know who are as a person. Your identity in Christ is the essence of your identity. Who you are in Christ will dictate the person you are and the person you continue to grow into. The way you carry yourself in Christ Jesus will be the same way you act in the world around you. Therefore, you must know and grow in Christ to know and grow thyself.

To the body of Christ and elected officials in the Black church, our main problems that arise are: Our identity in Christ is not respectable to our community and we have inaccurate teaching on the true identity of Jesus Christ to our people. It is insanity to think we can transform lives but not have proper relationships with Jesus Christ and not have an accurate understanding of the essence of God. Our reputation in our community is as follows: Pastors are whoremongers and hungry for the people's money, the church is all about self and church people are phony individuals who don't have any regard for truly living for Christ. Throughout a lifetime of observations, of conversations and cries of the people, it is a shame that as representatives of Christ we are not concerned with the image we put forth in our own community. As the Body of Christ, it's about winning souls and discipling others. We need to have a sense of urgency about winning people to Christ. You would think due to lockdowns in the Covid-19 pandemic we would have more and more urgency because we've had more time to think and reflect. We should be anxious to reach out to those who are not saved; instead, business carried on as usual, not having any regard for our fellow man. Life is about glorifying the Lord and not about living selfishly and foolishly.

The reason we play the fool is because we ourselves don't know God because we don't accurately know him through his word and personally from prayer and worship. Reading the Bible is key because it teaches us how to love God and how to follow his lead. The issue occurs when we are not trained and don't have the spirit to understand God. A lot of people who are operating as officials in the church aren't saved themselves, so there's no possible way they can help lead someone to salvation. Without being saved, trying to lead someone to salvation is like the blind leading the blind: Neither one of you will have any clue how to walk with Jesus. It is vital to be saved, filled with the Holy Spirit, because the Bible is written under the inspiration of the Holy Spirit (2 Timothy 3:16). Without salvation we don't have the Holy Spirit and without the Holy Spirit, it is extremely hard to accurately understand God. If you don't know God, the way to get to know him is through accepting his son Jesus Christ as Lord and Savior over your life and into your hearts. Repent of your sins, confess Jesus as Lord and Savior and believe in Jesus and you will be saved. Get saved; get the Holy Spirit and get understanding. Along with getting the Holy Spirit, revealing the true identity of God, get formal teaching about God's word. We cannot understand his word on our own; we need each other. Get to a church that is preaching and teaching the word of God in spirit and in truth. Go to Bible studies that break down the verses of scripture. Go to seminary, go to college, or go to classes your church offers that expound on reading the Bible. When you partake in one or more of those activities you can have a broad perspective on the characteristics of Jesus Christ and his will for your life. When you have that broad perspective then you can truly be effective in advancing the kingdom of God all over the earth.

Alongside learning the word of God, you have to have some intimacy with God. That intimate time is prayer and worship. Prayer and worship are the key ways to actively show that you know and love God. Prayer is our communication to God. Prayer will reveal what scripture means but God will direct your path in life when you talk to him. When you pray and listen God will speak back, giving you sound instruction. Our worship is vital because it is our adoration we have for God. Think of it like being married. Your spouse needs your attention through communication, because that's how you know the very thing that pleases your spouse. Your active compliments and praise are your adoration for your spouse. When you adore your spouse, it shows your gratitude for them and it is appreciated by them. The way we commune with a spouse or in any relationship is the same way we ought to do it toward God. Henceforth we must communicate and worship God to constantly build our relationship with him. Without a firsthand relationship with God, we can't be a testament to the world around us. To the Black church I urge you, get in right standing with God, so we can advance the kingdom of God and win souls unto God.

CHAPTER SIX

The Cry of the People "Looking for a Savior"

As a culture Black people in the United States and all over the world are in need of saving. We are tired; we are fed up with society treating us unjustly. As we view the news over the years, history shows us that society doesn't value the lives of Black people. Let's be honest with ourselves, America, how can you say Black Lives Matter when America habitually keeps repeating history? We as a people are still fighting the same fight in 2021 that our grandparents and great grandparents fought in 1961. In the 1950s and 1960s Blacks protested because of injustice and had dogs sicced on them or fire hoses sprayed at them, or were beaten by police. The story is still the same in the 2010s and 2020s. Now when we protest peacefully, tear gas is thrown at us. The reason we are even protesting is because we are tired of being killed by police, who are acting out of fear of Blacks and not out of rationality. We also protest for the mistreatment of Blacks in all avenues of life such as education, access to economic wealth, workplace misconduct, and the list goes on and on. So America, I propose this question: How can you say Black Lives Matter when you continually carry out the behaviors of your forefathers and habitually disrespect the existence of Black people? How can you say we matter but do us wrong every chance you get? An even better question to ask yourself, America: How can you say you love God but you don't even love Black people, who are also children of God? What God are you serving where you are trifling to a group of people? How is that even biblical to say you love all people but hate Blacks? How can you uphold biblical principles, America, but oppress an entire culture? Be real with yourselves, America, you are a wicked, perverse country who doesn't care about God. Therefore, I know you don't care about Black folk. Stop playing as if you are living for God with that hatred of Blacks in your heart. The Bible teaches us to have love for each other, because love will cover a multitude of sins (1 Peter 4:8). The exegesis of that text is, because we love each other we won't sin against one another and if we do sin against each other, we will do the right thing to make amends for the wrong

CHAPTER SIX

done. Unfortunately, the United States of America is too arrogant to love God so they are not going to love God's people. I urge you, America, repent of your sin and begin truly loving God and his people.

Due to always being treated unjustly Black people feel like we just can't come out victorious. Being Black in America can be overwhelming because of life's circumstances we are constantly overcoming, plus dealing with an unjust playing field because of the color of our skin. Sometimes you get frustrated with the fight of life but to all Black people, I encourage you to keep fighting.

The main difference in the fight now versus the fight in the 1960s is the church was there standing side by side with their people. Now, in the 2010s – 2020s, where are you church Negroes now. Negroes have their money and are nowhere to be found. Black people are looking for a savior. The Black church has the answer, which is Jesus, but don't care to present or represent Jesus. They'd rather be money-hungry, bloodthirsty pimps. The Black church in the 21st century is not any better than America oppressing Black people.

To the Black church, think about all we have been through as a people. At one point in history the Black

Church was there. In the time of the civil rights movement, we had Black church leaders like the Dr. Martin Luther King Jr. (Atlanta, Georgia), Dr. Rev. Samuel DeWitt-Proctor (Richmond, Virginia), Dr. Paritha Laura Ann Hall (Philadelphia, Pennsylvania), Octavia Albert (Georgia), Fannie Lou Hammer (Montgomery County, Mississippi), and Charles Albert Tindley (Berlin, Maryland – Eastern Shore), to name a few. Black pastors and other clergy walked side by side with their people. They followed God's lead, put their trust in the Lord and let God lead them to help liberate Black people. Black leaders fought the good fight of faith, while upholding righteousness until their time came to an end. They realized that it was needed to walk side by side with their people. Now, in the 21st century, we have issues just like before. We still deal with police brutality against Blacks such as cases like George Floyd (Minnesota), Sandra Bland (Texas), Breonna Taylor (Louisville, Kentucky), and Freddie Gray (Baltimore City, Maryland), just to list a few names to go along with the long list of murders that police in the United States are responsible for. In the midst of mass genocide of African Americans, whether it is from police or white supremacists, the Black church is absent in the fight for our lives.

CHAPTER SIX

Being Black in America, you basically have to be perfect because the rules of behavior are different for us than for our Caucasian counterparts. It seems like no matter how perfect we are we still suffer from injustice. Being Black, we can have all the education in the world and still find ourselves without work; we can protest peacefully and still be called hoodlums; we have the best credit in the world and try to get a loan to start a business to uplift our communities and we get denied. We are always put in denial in this country and all around the world. Our church leaders are still nowhere to be found; despite the injustice we constantly face. The Black community is crying out to be saved from this hell we are living on earth, we are crying out to be loved, and we are crying out to be supported.

Cry of Salvation:
The main cry for the Black community is the cry for salvation. All we want is to be liberated and to have freedom. We as a culture have dealt with oppression physically, mentally, emotionally and spiritually for over four hundred years. We are tired of being oppressed in every facet of life. As a people we desire to be liberated financially, theologically, judicially/ politically and psychologically. Those things have been historically constant restraints we have been dealing with.

Financially we have been burdened because we have habitually been denied access to wealth. We have been denied access to wealth because America simply doesn't want life for Blacks to be equitable and equal. If life is seen as equal and equitable then it means Blacks are truly equal and that they not only matter, but are worthy. If a system can oppress your access to finances, it can disrupt how you feel about your self-worth. As a culture we tie success to how we accumulate possessions rather than how our ancestors did, which was the sociological impact made on society. On the flip side of things, when the most important asset to survive other than Jesus is stolen from us it makes it hard to have an appreciation for life. Think about the situations in which the United States robs Blacks of wealth. In 1921 United States destroyed Black Wall Street in Tulsa, Oklahoma, because they were becoming the standard of success and America couldn't have that. You have everyday situations we encounter like being denied business loans that would grant us generational wealth. We are denied access to loans for homes; we are denied careers that would provide us with the means to take care of our families. We can apply for a career after graduating with a Bachelor's degree and be told we don't have the experience. We can get the experience plus more degrees and then be told we are overqualified. We

CHAPTER SIX

keep being denied access to wealth. Now to the Black community, all I can say is keep pushing for greatness. The road isn't fair, but we have to keep fighting. We don't have time to complain and lose hope; we must keep pushing. You don't need to steal and kill your way to the top. We have overcome with our minds. We must continue overcoming with our minds and faith in God. The best thing for our mind is to fix our eyes on Jesus. This walk is tough; it can be frustrating but, in the end, it's worth it, and you will win. To the Black church, stop manipulating the Black dollar for your selfish gain. Present Jesus and distribute wealth. The white church helps their community, no problem, the Asian church helps their own with no problem, but when it comes to the Black church we sit up and lie and say we can't do it. You can help your community overcome generational debt and help them prosper. Stop playing a liar and become the blessing God calls you to be. This is one of many ways God calls you to be a blessing. There have been many non-Christian organizations that have done more for the advancement of Black people than the so-called people of God. Due to non-Christian groups aiding the Black community, it puts Blacks in a position to ask why we even need the church. We have to do better representing God. If the people feel there is no need for church, they will feel no need for

God. The people will go to the ones that will help them achieve financial prosperity.

To the Black community, I urge you to be more responsible with your finances. As a people we have to start setting up future generations for financial blessings and not financial curses. Black people, stop using your money to flex your novice success to niggas that don't care about your existence. Stop wasting your money on trips you can't afford. Black queens, stop wasting your money on these negroes who are just in your life to use up your time, and all they have to offer is two minutes of sexual pleasure. To my Black kings, stop wasting your money to support women who are too lazy to work and would rather just use you as financial aid. In essence, as a community, we have to do better at managing money and looking out for family and community. We need to teach financial literacy to our community and keep passing on good financial practices from generation to generation. Most importantly, stop giving up on God when times get tough. God will provide. We have to seek Godly wisdom on how to handle money so we are not in a bind to begin with.

To the Black church, I urge you to stop robbing your community. The Black church is just as wicked as the

CHAPTER SIX

United States government with regard to stealing from the impoverished to feed the wealthy. In the church we come up with so many schemes to fill the pockets of the elect in church and do very little to support the community. You know people are struggling to pay bills, yet you will ask your people to sow a thousand-dollar seed and have the audacity to tell people watch God bless you as you sow this seed in faith. Stop using God to pimp out your own people. You can't predict and guarantee an exact behavior a person can do to be blessed. God blesses us sparingly. Our blessing isn't tied to one single action but to an overall relationship with him. If you want an accurate understanding of how to be blessed by God, read Deuteronomy 28:1-14. Therefore, my fellow saints in the Lord, educate your community accurately in how to deal with finances biblically. Keep it strictly Bible-based. An accurate understanding of God's will for how we should obtain money and utilize it will go a long way in our community. To liberate a community is to teach them the truth. The truth shall set us free.

The main thing to liberate people is the word of God. The Bible is essential in leading us to freedom. Unfortunately, we as a culture have been slaves to a mis-education in theology. On one side, dating back to slavery, we had our oppressors take scripture out of the Bible to manipulate African Americans to believe we were meant to be slaves and that it was ok. One another side we have our own church people enslaving us mentally, spiritually and emotionally with the word of God to have us live inaccurate lives just to please the wicked minds of the church elect. Think about all the times pastors/bishops have used the word of God to manipulate a crowd to do something, such as the scripture Luke 6:38, NKJV: "Give and it will be given to you: good measure pressed down, shaken together, and running over will be put into your bosom, For, with the same measure you use, it will be measured back to you." What Jesus is saying in context is the spirit in which you sow is the spirit in which it will be given back to you. Pastors will use this message in terms of giving of money for tithes and offerings. Pastors will manipulate that passage to get the congregation to give all their money, knowing people can't make rent, pay for food for their children, or send their children to college and much more. If you read the verses before and after you'll have an accurate understanding of the message Jesus is conveying to the people. A multitude of pastors using eisegesis and not exegesis leads to misuse of scripture, which eventually will lead to damaging lives of the people. To the pastors, I urge you to get the education and training on biblical preaching before you are in church shouting and talking about nothing. The souls of the people are at stake and it is imperative that you thoroughly know the word of God so you can help liberate a people and not enslave a people. To the Black church and Black community, it is just as imperative to learn the word of God and engage in extra study for yourself. You have to try the spirit by the spirit. You can't just take someone's word for scripture if you don't know it yourself. If you don't know it, learn some more and pray. If you seek God earnestly you will get the wisdom and understanding you need through scripture. When you have an accurate understanding of the word of God you can correctly apply it to your life. We have to understand that the pastor will be judged intensely for his doing but at the end of the day the desire to know God and follow Jesus is a decision you make and will be judged for. The first decision is to accept Jesus as Lord and Savior and then you have a daily decision to surrender your life, to follow Jesus, to trust him, to know him and love him every day. Joshua said it best in Joshua 24:15, in the middle of the verse: "choose for yourselves who you will serve." We have a choice to make every day in following the way of the Lord despite who the pastor may be. Choose for yourselves whether you're going with Jesus or not.

Once we stop robbing each other financially and theologically, we have to fight the good fight so we stop being robbed judicially and politically. In order to fight this fight, we have to stick together as a people. Stop creating division amongst one another. As Black people as a whole we tend to generate unnecessary troubles amongst ourselves. When Black people get saved and act holier than thou, they disregard the people on the outside. Black church folk dismiss the needs of the people and act like "that's not my problem, or I am not dealing with them niggas; they know better," the whole time forgetting you were just another nigga before you got saved. Just because you are saved doesn't mean you are any better than another person. Now Black people who aren't in church or even saved cause division because they say this Jesus stuff is the white man's religion. Black folk will read all these books on what it means to be Black, go to Black power seminars and call people coons for believing in Jesus. That ideology is an interesting one to partake in. For people to believe that Christianity is made up by white folk and is for white folk is quite absurd. How can a whole religion be made up by white people for white people and include a people who are geographically African, and have stories consisting of African people in power? One thing I learned about racist white folk: If they don't like you,

CHAPTER SIX

they're not going to include you. If anything, they will keep you excluded. Therefore, when society sees we can't agree on how we treat each other over differences in opinion then what makes you think they are going to respect us politically or judicially?

Let's keep it all the way one thousand. The justice system and politics are not meant to work in the favor of Black folk in this country. The United States doesn't give any cares in this world about Black folk having equal rights. Be real with yourself, America. How can you care about the advancement of Black people when you make rules and regulations that hinder Blacks from achieving the success they need to uplift their community, but will bypass those same regulations to help white folk who don't qualify to achieve success? Be real, America, you don't care about the Blacks in America; you just want to create the illusion that you do. The real reason you don't want Blacks successful is because if a Black person achieves greatness, it makes white supremacists mad because Blacks rise yet again despite roadblocks, when our white counterparts were given success and still failed. Just be honest, America, those are the games you play. America, stop letting the devil use you. All you're doing is bringing judgment to the land. Be honest and just.

There is politics in every avenue of Blacks trying to have equal rights. As Black people we are given less opportunity, scrutinized more, and criticized more harshly. Being Black in America, you have to be perfect; there is no room for error. Just to be safe we have to be perfect. When we are confronted by police, one wrong move and we are killed by police. Walk wearing a hoodie like Trayvon Martin did, and you can be killed. Only in America can negroes be killed and nothing happens, but when Asians get killed then President Joseph R. Biden (2021) makes a protective order for Asian Americans. I don't mean any harm but where is Black people's executive protection order. That's right—nowhere to be found. Even in the workplace we have to be perfect. A minor mistake at a job will get you fired. Then when you are devastated because of loss of employment it sets you up to be criticized as a failure. They say you weren't doing your job but the whole time they never provided you the resources to be successful. Let's not count the COVID-19 pandemic in 2020 and 2021, where oppressors tried to discredit the major effect that a pandemic has economically which will affect individuals' performances. Also, in politics we are not afforded the same opportunity to be efficient in office. We all remember President Barak H. Obama. He was highly criticized before the election and for

CHAPTER SIX

everything he did in his presidency. President Obama was the most criticized president ever, and had his peers work the most against him, and all he wanted to do was make America a better place. It was said he had no real experience in office, but he was a senator of an entire state. Throughout his terms in office, he couldn't catch a break. As Blacks we have to fight extremely hard to achieve success; meanwhile we will even have our own people fight against each other on what is important and not important. The important issue is we need saving and we need to work together.

When the politics are not in our favor, neither will the judicial system be in our favor. In school it's taught as checks and balances but when you look at the grand scheme of things it is the judicial system that operates the United States. What the law says goes. When whites commit a crime then an array of issues come to their defense as to why they committed a crime. The media will say things like he had a troubled past. His family was divorced, he was lonely with hardly any friends, so that's why he killed a bunch of people and then they send all these therapists the white folks' way because all they need is a talking-to. If a Black person commits a crime, the media will say they are savages; they are thugs; they live in a bad neighborhood and nothing good comes out of there. Being Black, when a crime is committed, then you are off to jail with the death penalty. How about this common scenario: Blacks getting stopped and then getting beaten by police to the point of death and then the cop gets paid leave and will eventually win the case. The disrespectful thing society will do is justify why it's ok to kill Blacks. This mentality is not acceptable, and these injustices make it more important to come together as a people. In order to fight the system, we have to be united in how we operate in this world and we must be willing to infiltrate the system. We need more Blacks to get into politics and the judicial system—not just any type of negro in office but one who truly values his or her community and that is not afraid to fight for their people. In order for this to happen we have to have people unified on various topics. A united Black community with the Black church backing it is a scary scenario for America. Until then we will keep going through the same nonsense that has plagued us for years. The only way to get that unity is to unify in Christ Jesus. Without Jesus we won't be victorious but with Jesus we have the victory.

Once we overcome the crisis politically and judicially then we can overcome the crisis of our mind. As a culture of Blacks in America we have been robbed of true

CHAPTER SIX

theology, economic wealth, equality in politics and in the judicial system, which in the end will lead to sociological and psychological torment.

As the world tunes in daily to the news you can see the prejudice against Blacks in the avenues mentioned above. As people you may question how we can overcome with so much against us. It just appears that no matter the education, no matter the credit score, no matter the qualifications, no matter the amount of money we have, and no matter if we have good character and a pure heart, it is not good enough to thrive in society.

Now society will throw minimal help our way and allow us as a community to experience minimal victories and then say, "See, we're not holding Black people back" and say, "Black lives matter." That is the problem right there, Black lives don't just matter; they are worthy. Little victories mean nothing if you are not thriving in life. All little victories do is just sedate the minds of the people to provide the illusion that life is progressing and is getting better. When you can get people to believe all is well, it makes people feel like there is hope and allows people to continue to live the lives they so desire. Black people, I encourage you to stop accepting the little things that society presents to you. It is the little things that show us how much the world around us values us as a people. It is evident every day that America and the world value us very little, if at all. For years we have constantly been oppressed, and it is burdensome to the mind. The human mind is not meant to live in oppression. There are only two options: fight and show how worthy you are or to give up because you feel like there is no hope.

The only real solution is to keep fighting. It is hard to fight a fight when depression rules your mind, when anxiety and fear keep you bound to nothingness, but nonetheless you have to keep pressing on and fighting the good fight. The only way to fight the good fight of faith is with Jesus on your side. This fight of injustice cannot be won alone; we must put our hope in a true savior. That true savior is Jesus Christ. Without Jesus, you will cause yourself to experience more psychological trauma, because you will cause yourself to run around in circles, which will result in increased depression, and can eventually lead to your destruction.

To the Black church, you have the resources needed to help the psyche of your people. Use the resources you have. The greatest resource is the Bible. Don't be clichéd in your rhetoric but truly give wise and Holy Spirit

CHAPTER SIX

lead counsel. Use proper hermeneutics to interpret and proper exegesis to explain the Bible and how to accurately understand the word of God and how to apply it to everyday living. Don't manipulate the minds of your people but better yet, heal the minds and the souls of the people. Black people are crying out for truth. The people are wounded and hurting because of the despair in life. Constant despair is overwhelming. Black people desire respect and to live peacefully. It's getting harder and harder to reach bliss on this side of glory because society doesn't value us. As a culture we're tired of having conversations with our kids that because the color of their skin the world will treat them differently. It is toxic to continue to live in fear and live not knowing if there is value in our lives. Black church, you are a part of the Black community; reach your people. Reach with genuine conversation through the Word and getting to know one another. Build relationships with your people. Formulate action plans to advance the betterment of Black people. Get involved in the community and love one another. Don't give up on your people. We are in this fight together, so don't have division among each other.

To the Black community on the outside looking in, stop discrediting help from the church when they do try to help, and allow yourselves to be open and free. Remain positive despite initial differences in opinion. Negativity is the very thing that hinders Black America from thriving in life. Don't harden your hearts to biblical counsel. Listen to the word of God, ask questions, get saved, get accurate understanding. When you harden your heart, you make it hard to grow as a people and hinder yourselves from experiencing true victory in Jesus. We need Jesus in the midst of everything to thrive in life. Don't be afraid to come together as a people. Let's come up with solutions together that make the world recognize the greatness in us. Let God's awesome power shine over us and through us.

CHAPTER SEVEN
Savior, Precious Savior: "The Solution"

As a people we are in need of saving. We live in an age where there is strife and tribulation on every side. Our hearts need saving. We as a culture are tired of mistreatment we receive on a daily basis. We are tired of white privilege and white supremacy having and taking precedence over Black lives. We are tired of a society valuing the color of a person rather than the heart and spirit of a person. We want respect, we want justice, we want love, and we want equity and equality in all facets of life. We fight every day for change in our society. We can't fight this fight alone. We need a savior, and that savior is Jesus. With Jesus on our side all things are possible. No matter if you're Black, Asian, White, Hispanic, East Indian, and everything in between, we need Jesus. Without having the spirit of Christ and the mind of Christ we can't make the world a better place. With Jesus we can be overcomers of the wickedness in this world.

Who is the Savior of the World?

In order to have a saving grace we need to know what or who is the saving grace we are seeking. You can't be saved without knowing the savior himself. That Savior is Jesus Christ our Lord. Jesus is the Son of God. He is a part of the Holy Trinity (Father, Son, Holy Spirit). Jesus is God's son, incarnated through the Virgin Mary. Jesus is God in the flesh. God came himself so he may identify with humanity and to show humanity how to live a life that is worthy. Let us just pause here—just ponder the thought of God himself coming in the flesh to identify with his creation and give us a direct example of how to live to please God. The most amazing thing a savior can do is come to identify with his people. We are to imitate Christ in our mannerisms. In order to mimic Christlike behavior, we needed the perfect example, and that example is Jesus. It doesn't get any better than to have someone to identify with the emotions, the thoughts, the affections and troubles we deal with, and to show us how handle life in a Godly way. Just take one moment to thank Jesus for coming down to earth to directly identify with us and show us the way to connect with his people, to show us that it is possible to live for holiness, and that it is possible to love unconditionally.

The same way Jesus came to identify with his people is the same way the Black church needs to identify with the community we serve. It is no longer good enough to sell gospel books, sell fish dinners, and hand out school supplies. We need a true connection between church and community. That connection must be authentic in every way. We have to be intentional in our love, and our love must be unconditional. To the Black people, in church or not in church, love must be unconditional. Love we have for one another must not know any limits. Limits must be taken off if we are going to break barriers. Limits have to be taken off so we can trust one another. We can't love if we don't trust each other. We have to have a Christlike mindset to serve one another. Jesus came that we may know him. As a people we don't know each other because we don't connect with one another. When we can connect with one another we can march on and fight the good fight of faith. When we connect, we can be victorious in life—not just crumbs of victory but monumental victories. We have to keep in the forefront of our minds John 10:10, that the devil will do all he can to steal, kill and destroy us but Jesus has already come so we may have life and have it to the fullest. We are meant to experience it in the fullness of God's goodness. Hence, we need Jesus. There is no other way to win but to come to Jesus (John 14: 6). To all, be open to Jesus; come to his family.

Why we need a savior in Jesus

The most common aanswer for the need for a savior is so we don't suffer God's wrath, judgment and hell for eternity. There is more to our need of a savior than just avoiding hellfire. Our need for a savior is that one be made alive and, be renewed, and it's a natural desire to want a saving grace.

Our initial problem at birth is being dead in our sin. We are naturally born into sin. We are born into sin because of the issues that have plagued our families over multiple generations. To overcome that sin in our lives we need a savior. That Savior which we seek is Jesus Christ our Lord. Without Jesus we are dead in our sin, meaning the sin in which we partake is our norm, and we see little to no harm in that sin. It is a harsh reality but the sins we have we tend to love, and we make the claim that "this is who I am." The problem with embracing your sin is you find no wrong in how you feel until it destroys your life and by that point it is too late. When you embrace your sin, you prioritize your sin over God. Sin will allow you to be selfish in your thinking and mannerisms. When sin is precedent in your life and is your norm, you will do anything to act on it without regard, and eventually that sin or sins will become an addiction and lead to your demise. Therefore, we need a savior to make us aware of our sin so we don't perish.

Too many of us are perishing in sin. We are letting our sin consume us to the point of death. When we reach the point of no return, we are no good to ourselves, our families and the communities in which we reside. When we are dead in sin, we miss out on serving God and reaping the blessings that God has for us. To my people, put your sin behind you and seek Jesus. We cannot afford to dwell in sin. It's our sins that keep destroying us individually and as a community. Our sins hinder us in our advancement as a people. We are so caught up in indulging in sin we can't seek righteousness, which would lead us to serving one another, and that would lead to the success of each other. When we put away our sin, we can genuinely love each other and look out for the best interest of each other.

To the Black church, present Jesus to your people; turn away from your sins of greed and lust. Your sins of greed and lust just echo back into the Black community and further damage it instead of uplifting it. To the Black community, you have to seek Jesus; leave these foreign gods alone. This idol and false god worshipping is killing you. When you worship other gods, it will allow further advancement of the sins you like to indulge in. As you continue to indulge in sin it pushes you farther away from God and hardens your heart. When it hardens your heart, it makes you have resentment toward the one and only true and living God, because now you realize your sins lead to your demise and now you have anger and pain living inside you. Accept Jesus as Lord and Savior to open your eyes to the things that are pleasing in the sight of the Lord. Allow Jesus to make you alive so you know sin and see the problem with sin and have a desire to live for righteousness and to have love. 1 Peter 4:8, NIV explains that "love covers over a multitude of sins," meaning that because you love God and desire God, you will turn away from your sins and do the appropriate things to live a life pleasing to King Jesus.

Another reason for soul salvation is to be renewed. After all the destructive behavior we heap on ourselves, whether from self-inflicted wounds or external wounds from sin,

CHAPTER SEVEN

we need redemption. Being redeemed by God is a fresh start, a second chance to live a better life. Sometimes even as believers in Jesus we need a second touch by God. In life we may be beaten down by the woes of life and become exhausted mentally, spiritually, and physically. We become so worn out by life it affects our mood, then our interactions will be affected and then our service for God becomes negatively affected. It is ok to get second chances in life. We all need a second chance at some point in our existence. We carry so many burdens we forget how blessed we are, we forget our purpose in life, we begin to lose sight of the missions we have in life and we ultimately end up frustrated and depressed. That depression eventually turns into extreme anxiety, which will make it hard to be effective in advancing the Kingdom of God. The good news is God can use anyone, but God desires your surrender so he can give you a second touch. God knows when to refresh your spirit. When God redeems you with his touch you become better than before. With a second touch from God, you have a renewed spirit, your wisdom increases, your application of the word improves, and you can get back to living productive lives for the Lord.

We also need a savior in Jesus because it is a natural affection that we wrestle with. Deep in our hearts, no matter how open or how stubborn we are, we still acknowledge that we need a savior. It is a natural affection to believe in something to be our saving grace in our lives. We have eternity tattooed on our hearts. As we ponder in our hearts, we know that there is a higher authority that keeps us safe and guides us, a power that is responsible for our existence and that is responsible for our eventual eternity. That power, that higher being, is God. The problem is we do everything in our power not to accept the deity of God. We desire God but we have internal issues that hinder us from completely surrendering and believing in God. We wrestle with our sin nature and the consequences of sin that keep us away from God. I want to encourage each and every one of you not to let the nature of sin hold you bound. God desires us to have a relationship with him. He put eternity in our hearts so that we will come to the realization that he wants us first and that's why we want him. It can be hard to surrender to something you only hear of and don't see, but that is the whole point of faith. Hebrews 11:1, NKJV says, "Faith is the substance of things hoped for, the evidence of things not seen." The whole point of faith in God is to trust in that which we don't see. The evidence of his work is good enough; it is to mold and build up our faith.

Ultimately, we are just human. We are with fault; we can't save ourselves. We fail ourselves, we fail each other, and over and over again we fail God when we don't have a connection to him. Jesus is that connection to God the Father. We have to accept Jesus Christ as Lord and Savior to have a relationship with the Father. With acceptance of Jesus, we are endowed with the Holy Spirit, which leads us in understanding of God and how to live a life pleasing to God. The Holy Spirit teaches, it convicts when we need conviction, it directs our paths, gives understanding and a whole host of attributes that help us draw closer to God. Open your minds, hearts, and souls to accepting Jesus so you can have a connection to God the Father and can live a life pleasing to him.

How can I obtain salvation?

Salvation is simple to obtain. You must confess with your mouth the Lord Jesus, and believe in your heart God raised Jesus from the dead and you will be saved (Romans 10:9). When you confess Jesus, it's making it known that this is the Savior that you believe in. The very thing you confess you typically will believe. Once the confession is made then the belief in the death and resurrection of Jesus is embedded in your heart. It is simply confessing and believing in Jesus. Don't let your own wisdom hinder you from knowing God. Be open and free in building your relationship with God. You don't have to be perfect; come as you are, with your faults, and allow God to mold you. Go after Jesus for yourself; be accountable for yourself. The church can't save you, only Jesus.

Final Exhortation to the Black Church and Community

To my people, I urge you to come and put your differences aside and let's have a conversation. To the Black church and Black community, let's have a seat at the table and let's get to know one another, to love one another and to have a true sense of unity with one another. Not all unions are perfect but the main thing unions have is respect, loyalty and love for one another. As a Black Union all over the world if we can come together and have the spirit of unity in love, respect and loyalty, we will do great things together. We have hurt each other long enough. Even in a pandemic we still choose to talk about one another and have lack of love for each other. God is calling us to greater things. God is calling us to be united. We as a union must find a way to come together. The only way we can come together is through Jesus. We as a people can no longer play the whore in society. Black church officials and Black church congregations, stop betraying your people to gain the riches of this world. Stop manipulating people to gain control over their lives, so you can have the upper hand over people, especially your people. Black church, preach Jesus; stop preaching hearsay to your communities. People need the true word of God; people need true worship; people need to know how to really live a life pleasing to God. Get educated on who God truly is and teach the Word in spirit and in truth.

The Covid-19 pandemic was a time for rest and to get back to God, not to continue with foolish behavior that is leading people to a devil's hell. In essence, be genuine in sharing the Gospel of Jesus Christ. Be examples of how to live a life pleasing to God. To the Black community, lean not on your own understanding of God (Proverbs 3:5-7). You need the Holy Spirit to fully understand God's word. You need the Holy Spirit to understand God's word because the Bible was written under the inspiration of the Holy Spirit (2 Timothy 3:16). In order to have the Holy Spirit you need to accept Jesus as your Lord and Savior. Repent of your sins, confess Jesus as Lord and Savior and believe, and you will be saved, and then comes the Holy Spirit. The

Holy Spirit will lead you in the way of everlasting life and a true relationship with Jesus. In order to get Jesus, let go of past hurt and frustration, be open and come willingly to Jesus. At the end of the day, no matter the hurt from other people, you are accountable for your own soul's salvation. To us all, we need Jesus. Get Jesus and don't turn back. Know Jesus, know love. God bless and I love you all.

ABOUT THE AUTHOR

Vaughn Lee Adams Jr, also known as J.R., is the son of Reverend Vaughn Lee Adams Sr. of Salisbury, Maryland, and Linda (Young) Adams of Philadelphia, Pennsylvania. J.R. comes from a long line of Pastors, and Deacons on both sides of his family, that came from the West Indies to the United States. The call to service reigns supreme through his grandparents and parents.

J.R. grew up learning about the Lord at the young age of four years old. His parents instilled in him the importance of salvation, and having a relationship with Jesus. It wasn't until 2013 that J.R. accepted Jesus Christ as Lord and Savior. J.R. was 26 years old, he has been on fire for the Lord since then. After salvation, during undergraduate studies at the University of Maryland Eastern Shore, he was a member on the events board of Praise Fellowship, serving as a Bible Study teacher for Praise Fellowship and its sub group Bold Brothers. He was crowned Mr. Praise Fellowship, representing Praise Fellowship at the Annual Coronation at UMES. At UMES he was also the historian for Exercise Science club.

J.R. was also licensed as a Minister from Greater New Hope Church and Ministries (Preston, Maryland) October 2016. After Graduation he served as the Academic Advisor for Praise Fellowship at UMES from 2017-2020, and was also a Volunteer Track Coach at UMES 2019-2020.

J.R. has a beautiful fiancé, whom he will be married to on October 10, 2021, Cierre and son, Jayden whom he loves and adores.

www.ingramcontent.com/pod-product-compliance
Lightning Source LLC
Chambersburg PA
CBHW070322100426
42743CB00011B/2524